Important Notice:

ONLY eat plants that you clearly recognize
and know to be clean, chemical free
and in plentiful supply.

Use all your senses when identifying plants but
especially your sense of smell.

www.eatingflowers.com
www.plantlife.org.uk
www.soilassociation.org

CONTENTS

Preface   5

March   Nettle & Sweetcorn Fritters   9
Nettle   Nettle Soup   11
                 Nettle Omelette   13

April   Wild Garlic on Toast*   17
Wild Garlic   Golden Garlic Potatoes   19
                 Wild Garlic Sandwich*   21

May   Petal Pancake*   25
Hawthorn   Hawthorn Roly Poly*   27
                 Beetroot & Hawthorn Salad   29

June   Elderflower Ice Lollies*   33
Elderflower   Elderflower Cordial & Jelly   33
                 Baked Salmon*   35
                 Rhubarb & Elderflower Jam   37

July   Scones with Rose Cream   41
Roses   Rose Ice Cream   43
                 Rose Castles*   45
                 Rose Vinegar*   45

August   Nasturtium Pasta*   49
Nasturtiums   Leaf Parcels   51
                 Stuffed Nasturtiums*   53

September   Peanut Butter Biscuits   57
Lavender   Lavender Almond Biscuits   57
                 Lavender Lemonade   59
                 Trapped Beauties*   61
                 Ice Flower Bowl   61

October   Chocolate Crispies*   65
Dandelion   Dream Bread Pudding*   67
                 Dandelion Salad*   69
                 A List of Edible Flowers   71

*The recipes marked * are easiest to make.*

First published in 2011 in Great Britain by
Dellipress Ltd.
4 Dolphin Street
Deal CT14 6LX

ISBN 978 0 9570974 0 7

NOTE: The material contained in this book is for general guidance and no liability can be accepted for mistaken identity of any of the plants. The use of any information contained in this book is entirely at the reader's own risk.

Preface

Listen to the bees and feel the sun on your back whilst gathering dandelions, rose petals, and garlic leaves? Wandering about in the wild from a young age can bring happiness that lasts all one's life. If you know what to pick and eat then even better!

In the 21st century as we plug into technology let us not unplug from nature. Teach yourself the joys of using plants and leaves throughout the year in delicious recipes. Goodbye processed food!

Throughout the 1990's I ran a cafe, *The Cafe du Livre* in South West France. One day a little old widower shuffled in with a baguette tucked under his arm. The other hand held a bunch of vervain cut from his terrace - the first wild delicacy had arrived. Soon we were identifying all manner of hedgerow bounty including a cafe favourite, *Sirop de fleur de Sureau, p. 33.*

Food is medicine. Wild food is packed with untold goodness. Every Spring I grab a basket and pick young nettle leaves. The soup is truly delicious and nourishing. Bon Appetit!

Lucia Stuart,
Hay-on-Wye.
October 2011.

MARCH

Nettle (*Uritca dioica*) fritters, page 9.

a juicy nettle leaf

Nettles grow happily in the damp British climate.
Look for them in wasteland and overgrown areas.
Always wear rubber gloves to pick them because
the leaves sting. The Victorians liked eating them
so much they were sold in bunches at the market.

HOW TO EAT: Cook the leaves first. The sting
instantly vanishes. They are packed with vitamins,
minerals and protein to revitalize us after a long
damp winter. Nettles are delicious in gnocci,
risotto, lasagne, ravioli stuffing, curries and pies.

Protein per 100g = 5.9g *compared to the highest vegetable: Kale = 3.0g*
Vitamin C per 100g = 333mg *compared to lettuce = 13mg.* Vitamin A per
100g = 740mg. For the intrepid, brush your arthritic joints regularly
through nettles; the stings have been known to improve the condition.

Nettle + Sweetcorn Fritters

Mix to a thick cream:

a pinch of salt

Nettle & Sweetcorn Fritters

See the photograph on page 6. Makes 6 fritters.
In a bowl make some batter. Mix together:

1 egg
a pinch of salt
3 tablespoons of flour
5 tablespoons of tinned sweetcorn
6 tablespoons of nettle leaves:
boiled, drained & chopped up.

It should be a gloopy paste. Add a drop of
warm water or flour if necessary.

Put 5 spoons of olive oil into a frying pan and
heat until the oil is smoking. Beware of the
spluttering oil as you place a spoon of the
fritter mixture into frying pan to make a little
cake. Add 2 more fritters to the pan. Press
them down and cook until they are crispy
golden on one side, about 4 minutes. Flip
them over and cook the other side. Place the
fritters on kitchen paper to absorb excess oil.

Eat them hot with harrissa if you like chilli,
or dip them into creamy Greek yogurt.

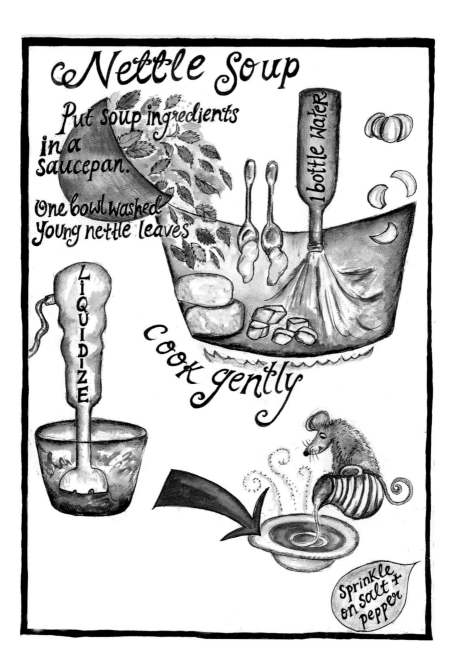

Nettle Soup

potatoes
double cream
water or stock
unsalted butter
garlic (pink, french is best)
nettle leaves - no stalks or stems

Wearing gloves wash a bagful of young nettle leaves; the top leaves of about 25 stems. Omit all veins and stalks. Leave them to dry.

Peel 2 medium-large potatoes. Chop into chunks. Peel and slice 3 cloves of garlic. Put 2 spoons of unsalted butter into a thick saucepan. Fry the garlic and potato in the butter with a lid, stirring often, for about 7 minutes.

Add the nettles for a further 5 minutes. Stir. Lastly pour in 1 litre of stock or water. Simmer gently for 30 minutes.

Liquidize the soup. Taste and season accordingly. Reheat and ladle it into bowls with double cream swirled on top. My brother loves a dash of Tabasco sauce.

NOTE: *To make the soup ultra smooth sieve it after liquidizing.*

Nettle Omelette

OUCH!

cumin seeds

Pour into a thick frying pan

cheese

Then put under the grill to puff up for 5 mins.

EAT WARM OR COLD.

Nettle Omelette

*salt
eggs
onion
olive oil
cumin seeds
nettle leaves
halloumi cheese*

Put 2 mugs of washed nettle leaves into a small saucepan. Boil them for 3 minutes. Drain and when they are cool squeeze them dry with your fingers and tear up the leaves.

Separate 5 egg whites and yolks. Tip the whites into one bowl and yolks into another.

Fry 1 teaspoon of cumin seeds in a dry frying pan for a minute then stir in 4 spoons of olive oil and 1 diced onion. Cook stirring, for a couple of minutes and then turn off the heat.

Whip the egg whites with an electric beater until they stand in peaks. Add the whites to the yolks carefully retaining the air for fluffiness.

Add the nettles, half a mug of diced halloumi cheese, the onions, cumin and a pinch of salt.

Pour everything into the warm frying pan and cook for 25 minutes. Putting it under the grill for a couple of minutes will make the top go golden. Otherwise, simply cool and unstick the omelette with a knife. Then turn it upside down onto a plate.

APRIL

Wild garlic (*allium ursinum*) growing in shady woodland.

Opposite: *Fried potatoes with nutmeg and garlic leaves p.19.*

Wild garlic grows close together like a carpet in moist woods and shady hedgerows. The flower is white and star shaped amidst leaves that are shiny, smooth and soft. It tastes like a garlic-infused spinach leaf and has a short season. The strong smells aids identification.

HOW TO EAT: The whole leaf can be eaten raw or cooked. Wipe it clean first. Use it as you would baby spinach, tossing it into hot pasta and salads. Use the leaves to make 'pesto' crushing them to a paste with walnuts and olive oil or add them to bechamel sauce.

If you suffer from Hay fever or sinusitis eat a few flower heads. They taste stronger than the leaves and may well help the problem. Wild garlic lowers blood pressure and cholesterol.

A Wild Garlic Toastie

Wild Garlic on Toast

bread
butter
cheese
tomato
wild garlic leaves

Grill two slices of bread on one side.
Butter the untoasted side.

Tear 6 garlic leaves in half. Discard the
stems. Place the leaves on top of the
butter. Cover them with 3 slices of ripe
tomato followed by 2 slices of cheese.

Place the toastie under the grill until the
tomato is soft and the cheese has melted
and is golden.

Golden Garlic Potatoes

A lid will help the cooking process.

Golden Garlic Potatoes

nutmeg
potatoes
salt & pepper.
wild garlic leaves
walnut oil or olive oil

See the photograph on page 15. Scrub 3 medium-sized potatoes and cut them into small cubes.

Put 5 spoons of oil into a thick frying pan. When it is very hot add the diced potatoes. Cook over a medium-hot flame with a lid on, stirring.

After 15 minutes add a tablespoon of freshly grated nutmeg and a pinch of salt and pepper.

Wipe clean 6 garlic leaves per person. Remove the stalks and tear each one into 3. Add to the hot potatoes. Cook for a further few minutes, stirring. The potatoes are cooked when they are soft. Taste for seasoning and adjust accordingly.

NOTE: To make this dish into a main course add cubes of cheese to the potatoes just before serving. It will melt and ooze about deliciously.

Wild Garlic Sandwich

OI, TEA'S READY!

A Wild Garlic Sandwich

bread
butter
garlic leaves
cream cheese

Butter 2 slices of bread and spread
them with a favourite filling such as
cream cheese, tuna fish or salmon.

Lay some clean, torn up garlic leaves
on the filling followed by a second
slice of buttered bread. Tuck in!

MAY

Hawthorn *(crataegus monogyna)* roly poly, page 27.

Hawthorn branches have sharp thorns which helps one to recognise the tree. The young leaves have a nutty taste and the blossom smells sweet. In Autumn crimson berries, or haws, abound. These can be used for jam or drink making but they are probably most enjoyed by the birds because of their large seeds.

HOW TO EAT: Nibble upon the young leaves. The white blossom and pinkish white buds have a delicate almond flavour. *(Below Sheep sheltering under a Hawthorn tree, in Caemaw Meadow, Hay-on-Wye.)*

This ancient tree heals the heart. The berries and leaves are used for the physical heart by regulating both high and low blood pressure. The flowers ease heartbreak.

Petal Pancakes

Mix up the eggs and flour

Add the milk drop by drop so it is like thick cream.

Try tossing it over in the air

Sprinkle with lemon juice, sugar + petals

Petal Pancakes

eggs
milk
butter
plain flour
hawthorn flowers
lemon juice & sugar

This recipe makes 5 pancakes. To make the batter put 6 tablespoons of flour into a mixing bowl. Make a well in the centre and crack in 2 eggs. Draw the flour into the egg from around the edge of the bowl making a thick paste. Then slowly add drops of milk and stir to make it the consistency of double cream.

Put two spoons of butter into a frying pan. When it smokes use a ladle or jug to pour enough batter into the frying pan to make a thin layer. Tilt it around quickly until it spreads out evenly.

When the pancake is solid and the sides curl up, loosen it with a spatula. Toss it over and cook the other side. The first pancake is usually a wonky one. Keep going - practice makes perfect.

Sprinkle the pancake with sugar, lemon juice, hawthorn or other spring flowers: primroses, violets, primulas, clover flowers, pansies or broom buds.

Hawthorn Roly Poly

Hawthorn Roly Poly

See the photograph on page 22. Preheat the oven to
375° F/ gas mark 5. In a bowl make the suet pastry.

Mix together:
1 mug of plain flour
half a mug of vegetable suet
1 teaspoon of baking powder

Add cold water so that it comes together to make a
soft ball. Knead gently to incorporate air.

Sprinkle flour onto the table and rolling pin.
Roll the suet into a rectangle about 1 cm thick.
Place it on some buttered greaseproof paper.
Spread the top with a few spoons of homemade
jam and sprinkle over a handful of young
hawthorn leaves. Roll it up carefully.

Bake it for 20 minutes in the pre-heated oven. Cut
the warm roly poly into slices. Serve with custard.

NOTE: *To make a blackberry roly poly*: sprinkle the
suet with blackberries and fresh mint leaves.
To make a savoury one: sprinkle over bacon and
hawthorne leaves. Serve with gravy or tomato
sauce.

Beetroot + Hawthorn Salad

Hawthorn Buds and flowers

Beetroot Hawthorn Salad

olive oil
beetroot
salt and pepper
balsamic vinegar
thick greek yogurt
watercress or wild garlic leaves
young hawthorn buds & flowers

Scrub 1 beetroot per person under a cold tap. Cut off the leaf tops. Boil them in a saucepan of water with a lid for 25 minutes. Remove and cool.

Toss the clean watercress in a little balsamic vinegar mixed with olive oil. Arrange it on a large serving plate. Peel and slice the cooked beetroot into discs. Arrange them on top of the watercress.

Mix together: 2 spoons of olive oil,
                    salt & pepper
                    4 tablespoons of yogurt.

Spoon the dressing over the beetroot and sprinkle over the pinky white, almond-tasting hawthorn flowers and buds.

JUNE

Homemade elderflower (*sambucus nigra*) ice lolly, page 33.

Elder is a leafy tree that grows in rough ground. It thrives in fields and towns. The creamy white flowers smell strong. Do not wash them as the fragrance may go. Shake clean to remove dust and insects. The dark purple berries vary in taste but can be a worthwhile cooking ingredient.

HOW TO EAT: Eat the white blossom. It tastes as if fruit and flowers were mixed together. Use elderflowers to infuse a delicate flavour into food and drink; such as, elderflower and rhubarb ripple ice cream or elderflower and gooseberry pie.

Elderflowers are anti inflammatory and soothing for hay fever which coincides with their blooming. The berries are full of immune boosting Vitamin C and arrive just in time to fight winter ailments.

Elderflower ice lollies

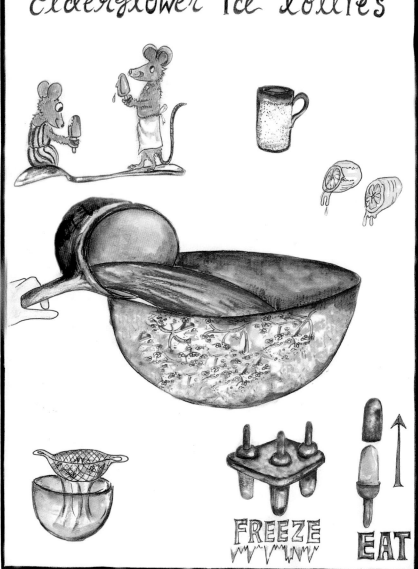

Elderflower Ice Lollies

sugar
lemons
elderflower blossoms
ice lolly moulds obtained from kitchen shops.

See the photograph on page 30. Put 2 mugs of sugar and
2 mugs of water into a thick saucepan and heat
slowly to dissolve the sugar. Boil the liquid for 3
minutes. Pour it into a ceramic bowl on top of 20
fragrant elderflower blossoms. Add the juice &
grated rind of 2 lemons. Cover and leave to cool.

Sieve the liquid. Pour it into ice lolly moulds. Place
them in the freezer to harden.

NOTE: *To make a tub of sorbet pour the liquid into one
plastic container and freeze. When it is nearly frozen whisk
in 1 or 2 whipped egg whites and freeze until hard.*

Elderflower Cordial or 'Sirop de Fleur de Sureau'

sugar
water
elderflower blossoms

Pack a large bowl with sprays of young fragrant
elderflower blossoms. Pour over 2 litres of water to
submerge them. Leave for 24 hours.

Taste the water. It should be flowery. (Add more
flowers to strengthen the flavour if necessary).

Sieve it into a pan with 3 mugs of caster sugar and
put it on a medium heat. Dissolve the sugar and
simmer for 5 minutes to make a thin syrup. Cool
and bottle. For longevity store in a cool dark place.
Before drinking, dilute it with cold water to taste.

Salmon Baked with Elderflowers

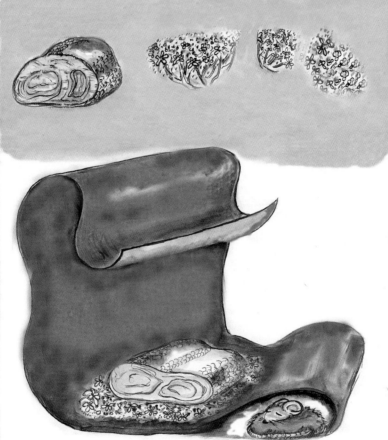

Bake the fish in a hot oven for 12 minutes.

Baked Salmon

butter
fresh salmon
elderflower blossom
vinegar or white wine

Preheat the oven to Gas 5 or 370° F.

Rub some butter on a piece of silver foil. Place 5 bunches of elderflower blossoms on the foil followed by 1 salmon steak per person on top of the elderflowers. Add a tablespoon of vinegar or white wine.

Seal the edges of the foil to make a loosely wrapped, tight parcel. (You can also make a greaseproof paper parcel). Place it in the warm oven for 12 minutes.

NOTE: *For a winter version cut a washed leek into thin slices. Place the salmon on top and bake as above.*

Elderflower & Rhubarb Jam

The Secret of Successful Jam

Make small quantities.

use a thick Saucepan so that the sugar does not burn

Rhubarb & Elderflower Jam

rhubarb
caster sugar
elderflowers - the white petals only

Clean and chop some rhubarb into chunks.
Measure 4 heaped mugs of rhubarb and 5 mugs
of sugar into a thick saucepan. Heat slowly.

After 20 minutes check that the sugar has
dissolved. The bottom of the pan should not be
gritty. Simmer the jam gently for about 40
minutes. If it is sticky when cool then it is ready.
If not, continue cooking for a little longer.

Stir 1 mug of white elderflower petals into the
jam omitting any stalks. They should be dry,
fresh and fragrant.

Sterilize the jam jars by covering them with
boiling water from the kettle. Dry them and
ladle in the jam. Seal and store the jars upside
down to prevent air entering. Store in the dark.

NOTE: *Try the jam to accompany savoury dishes*
such as duck, fresh mackerel or cheese & crackers.

JULY

Scones with rose *(rosa)* petal cream, page 41.

Rose Petal Sugar: Whizz up some throughly
dried rose petals with granulated sugar 1:3
for a fragrant floral sweetener.

The Rose is 5,000 years old first hailing from Asia Minor. The more heavily scented a rose, the stronger the taste will be. When you find a plump fragrant rose cut it from the bush using scissors.

HOW TO EAT: Eat the petals but ensure they have not been chemically treated. *See sugar recipe opposite* The rose hip, a redish berry-like fruit, attaches to the rose tree for months. The flesh is full of Vitamin C and the seeds Vitamin A. For syrup: liquidize then sieve mature hips, to remove the inedible hairs.

Rose hips have more Vitamin C than any citrus fruit. Rose hip powder has been shown to reduce osteoarthritis and stiffness and pain in joints. Rosewater cleanses and soothes skin.

Scones with Rose Petal cream
using finger tips rub
BUTTER
x2
1 mug of flour
baking powder
use a scone cutter

Rose Cream Scones

See the photograph on page 38.
Makes 20 scones. Preheat the oven to 350°F/ gas 4.
You will need a fluted, tall-sided 2' scone cutter.

In a bowl put: *a heaped mug (200g) of flour*
                  2 tablespoons of unsalted butter (45g)
                  ½ teaspoon of salt,
                  1 tablespoon of baking powder
                  2 teaspoons of caster sugar

Rub the butter into the flour using the tips of your
fingers. Use a metal spoon to stir in enough *whole milk*
(150ml) to make a dough that becomes a soft, cold
moist ball. Handle it very gently. *Taste to check that the*
sugar & salt balance is correct - add more of it if necessary.

Sprinkle the table, rolling pin and the scone cutter with
flour. Endeavour to trap air in the pastry as you fold
and roll it out to ¾ inch thick. Use the cutter, to cut out
the scones. Bake in the warm oven on a greased tray.

After 10/12 minutes they should be puffed up and
golden underneath. They should be light and soft.

To eat them, cut the scone in half and spread each side
with rose cream *(or butter)* followed by homemade jam.

I have fond memories of demonstrating 'how to eat an English
scone' to French customers. We had a blackboard in the cafe to
explain the technique - the origin of this book perhaps? You
cannot get scone cutters abroad, so I often travel with one

Rose Cream: Tear some strongly scented rose petals
into a small bowl of whipped cream. Add a few drops of
Rose water and a tiny drop of red food colouring.

Rose Ice Cream

Rose Ice Cream

Ensure the rose is very fragrant, clean and
unsprayed. Into an electric mixer whizz up:

> *petals from 1 or 2 large fragrant roses*
> *1 tub of thick greek yogurt.*
> *2 tablespoons of sugar or icing sugar*

Ladle the ice cream into individual glass
dishes and leave them in the freezer for
several hours to set hard.

15 minutes before eating the ice cream
remove it from the freezer so that it softens.

Rose Orange Ice Cream

Fill an orange with the rose ice cream. Cut the
top off a clean orange. Scoop out the inside.
Discard it. Grate some orange rind into the
ice cream plus a tiny drop of *red food colouring.*

Fill the empty orange with the ice cream.
Replace the top of the orange and freeze it.

Rose Castles

peel off any surrounding paper

Rose Castles

petite suisse - fromage frais
rose petals and small berries
honey, golden or maple syrup

Remove the lid from the tub of petite suisse.
Invert it onto a plate. Tap and squeeze it gently
so that it slips out of the plastic container.
Remove the paper wrapping.

Decorate 'the castle' with petals, berries and
dribbles of honey or syrup. *This is ideal dish for*
encouraging very young children into the kitchen.

Rose Vinegar

Scented vinegars are a interesting ingredient to have
in the kitchen to use in sauces, gravies & vinagrettes.

Loosely fill a wide necked bottle with rose
petals. Top the bottle up with good quality
vinegar. Place the jar in the sun for 3 or 4 weeks
rotating regularly. Drain and store.

NOTE: *Other good vinegar flavours are: fennel*
flowers, tarragon, raspberries, elderflower, mint.
You can use the same principle to make flavoured olive
oil using basil, chilli, lavender and so on.

AUGUST

Multi-nutritious nasturtiums (*tropaeolum majus*), page 49.

Nasturtiums grow in trails, tumbling over garden walls in a tangle. Their trumpet-like flowers are red, yellow and orange. The leaves are soft and round with a peppery spicy flavour which adds zap to cooking. They contain lots of Vitamin C.

HOW TO EAT: Munch the leaves and flowers raw in salads. The flower seeds which look similar to capers can also be eaten. Pickle them in brine.

Originally from Peru the flaming flowers were adopted by the Spanish in the 16th century and were used for preventing scurvy. The seeds are antiseptic/antibacterial.

Nasturtium Pasta Ribbons

Drain

Add enough cheese & cream to coat the Pasta

Sprinkle with torn up Nasturtium flowers & leaves

Nasturtium Pasta

onion
cheese
double cream
nutmeg & cloves
tagliatelle pasta
nasturtium flowers & leaves

See the photograph on page 46.
Push 6 cloves into a peeled onion and
submerge in a large saucepan of cold salty
water. When the water boils add 75g tagliatelle
per person. Cook for 10 minutes or so
depending on the amount of pasta you use.
Bite the pasta to see if it is cooked through.

Drain the pasta and return it to the warm
saucepan. Discard the onion.

Add 1 teaspoon of grated nutmeg, a mugful of
grated cheese and a splash of double cream.
Put the pan back on a low heat, stirring well
for a few minutes to melt everything together.

Tip the creamy pasta onto a warm plate and
sprinkle it with nasturtium leaves and flowers.

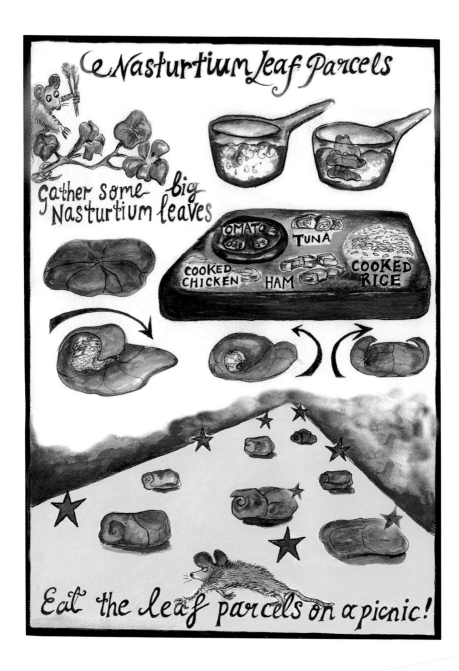

Leaf Parcels

salt
cooked basmati rice
big nasturtium leaves
chopped: tuna, tomato,
ham, roast chicken

Gather 7 big nasturtium leaves. Put them
in a saucepan with a mugful of salty water.
Simmer for 2 minutes. Drain and pat dry.

In the middle of the leaf put a teaspoon
of whatever takes your fancy: cooked rice,
chicken, tuna, chopped tomato, herbs.

Wrap it up to make a little green parcel.
As in the drawing opposite. Pat olive oil
around the edges to help it stick together.

Serve the leaf parcels decorated with
nasturtium flowers.

Stuffed Nasturtiums

CREAM

Chives   Mint   Parsley   Basil

Nasturtium flowers

WATCH OUT MICE ABOUT!

Stuffed Nasturtiums

salt
cream cheese
double cream
nasturtium flowers
chopped fresh herbs

Pick several large nasturtium flowers and check
they are clean. Shake off any dust.

In a bowl mix 3 teaspoons of cream cheese with
2 teaspoons of double cream. Add some finely
chopped herbs: mint, basil, dill, lovage or
chives and pinch of salt. Taste the mixture.

Hold a nasturtium flower with one hand and
fill it with a teaspoon of the herb mixture.

Arrange them on a plate to accompany drinks..

SEPTEMBER

Lavender flowers (*lavandula angustifolia*) are a fragrant cooking
ingredient for sweet and savoury dishes.

Opposite: *Lavender Almond biscuits p.57.*

Lavender flowers are purple with pointed grey green leaves. They belong to the *labiates* - 'lipped' flowers with a mouth that one can pull open and a hanging lower lip. Sage and Rosemary are in this group. The plant prefers a dry climate and grows happily in chalky soil and sunshine.

HOW TO EAT: Eat the purple flowers fresh or dried. Sprinkle on salads or in cakes and biscuits. Grind them up with lemon zest, cumin and coriander seeds and rub onto duck breasts or quail prior to roasting.

Rub a little lavender oil on your skin if you have burns or sunburn. It is also good for stings and repels insects. Sprinkle some oil on bed linen for nocturnal relaxation.

Peanut Butter Biscuits

Makes 12 biscuits. Preheat the oven to gas 4 or 350°F.
In a bowl mix together:

1 egg
½ mug of caster sugar (100g)
3 teaspoons of lavender flowers
3 teaspoons of vanilla essence
1 small jar of crunchy peanut butter

Form 12 walnut-sized balls with your hands. Cold
water will prevent stickiness. Lay them on a buttered
baking tray. Press them down gently with a small fork.
Bake them for 17 minutes until golden brown.
Remove from the paper when cool and hard.

Lavender Almond Biscuits

See the photograph on page 55. Makes 20 biscuits.
Preheat the oven to gas 4 or 350°F.
Into an electric mixer put:

half a pat of unsalted butter (125g)
a mug of plain flour (150g)
a mug of ground almonds (200g)
½ a mug of soft brown sugar (100g)
5 lavender flowers no stem

Whizz everything up until it sticks together. Squeeze
and roll small balls. Lay them on buttered greaseproof
paper. Press them down with a fork to make biscuits.
Bake in the oven for about 15 minutes until they are
pale golden beige and look cooked. Wait until they are
cool before peeling them off the paper.

*NOTE: If you use too much lavender in dishes it can taste
bitter and soapy instead of herby and perfumed. Taste the
biscuit mixture is just right before cooking.*

Lavender Lemonade

1 litre of Water

leave Covered Overnight

SUGAR

Lavender Lemonade

Lavender Lemonade

water
lavender flowers
granulated sugar
3 lemons, preferably unwaxed organic

Peel 3 lemons avoiding the pith. Halve the lemons and squeeze out the juice.

Put the peel, juice and lemon halves in a bowl with 2 litres of water. Add 25 to 30 clean, fragrant lavender flowers.

Cover the bowl and leave it overnight.

Sieve the mixture into a saucepan, pressing the lemons and flowers to extract flavour. Add 3 mugs of sugar (800g).

Heat the liquid so that the sugar dissolves first. Simmer it for 2 minutes. Cool and use a funnel to decant it into clean bottles.

Before drinking dilute it to taste with ice cold water. It has the delicious taste of homemade lemonade with a floral back note.

NOTE: *Do not throw the lemon husks away. Place them in an area that smells bad such as a fridge and they will dispel the odours immediately.*

Trapped Beauties

Primrose
Petals

Dandelion
Petals

Sweet
Williams

flowers

Mint
leaves

berries

Trapped Beauties

water
edible flowers & leaves
i.e. violet, lavender, rose, borage.

Arrange the flowers in the compartments of an ice tray. Pour over cold water and place them in the freezer.

Ice Flower Bowl

water
beautiful petals & leaves
2 bowls & some sellotape

.

Find 2 bowls that fit together with a space in between. *(I used 2 china christmas pudding bowls).* ⅓ fill one bowl with cold water and add lots of small delicate flowers and petals: violas, sweet williams. roses etc. Be generous with the flowers. Pack them in! They will float up the sides from the bottom.

Float the smaller bowl on top. Use tape and/or a weight to press it down and hold it in place so that the water sandwiched between comes up to the rim. Top it up with water and flowers if necessary.

Place in the freezer for a few hours. When the ice bowl is frozen hard, dislodge it by applying very hot water with a cloth to the outer bowls and wait. Be patient. I recommend practicing this delightful creation before you make an official presentation.

OCTOBER

Gathering dandelion flowers *(taraxacum officinale)* for pudding, page 67.
Leaves growing in the shade taste sweeter than those in the sun.

Opposite: *Dandelion salad with wild strawberries p.69.*

Dandelions have yellow flowers and jagged leaves
resembling lion's teeth, 'dent-de-lion'. They grow in
open grassy fields with their flowers facing the sun.
The seed head, which resembles a puff of cotton
wool is a magnificent feast for the birds.

HOW TO EAT: Eat the young leaves which taste
bitter but are good for the liver and kidneys. Chop
them finely. They add flavour to rice and noodle
salads. The petals can be used for wine-making. The
dried root makes a satisfactory coffee substitute.

Dandelion is one of the top 6 herbs in the Chinese herbal medicine
chest. It contains more vitamin A than anything else apart from fish
oil and liver. It is a cocktail of pure goodness for a human organism.

Chocolate Flower Crispies

Stir over a low heat

YUM! YUM!

Leave the cakes to cool in the fridge

Chocolate Crispies

chocolate
a dandelion
unsalted butter
raisins or sultanas
cornflakes or other cereal

See the photograph on page 70.
Make a bain-marie to melt the chocolate. Fit a
mixing bowl into a saucepan of water. Lift the
bowl off and the water should reach half way up
the outside of the bowl. Place the pan on heat.

Break one large bar of chocolate into the bowl.
Add 2 tablespoons of unsalted butter. Stir.

When the chocolate is melted remove it from
the heat. Stir in 2 cups of cornflakes or rice
crispies and 3 tablespoons of raisins or sultanas.

Spoon the mixture into paper cases or a cake tin
to make small individual heaped-up crispies.
Place a dandelion on the top of each cake.*

Put the chocolate crispies in the fridge to cool.

* Or *decorate the cakes with whatever edible flowers
you have: primulas, common mallow etc. See page 71.*

Dream Bread

2 Spoons milk

Prepare the bread

maple Syrup

Mmm

Dandelion Dream Bread Pudding

eggs
milk
butter
white bread
syrup or honey
dandelion petals
fino sherry (optional)

Crack 2 eggs into a mixing bowl with 2 tablespoons of milk. Beat up with a fork. Snip some dandelion petals into the mixture.

Remove the crusts from a slice of bread and cut it into 3 fingers.

Melt 4 tablespoons (50g) of butter in a frying pan. When it is hot and brown, dip a bread finger into the egg mixture and fry it on each side until it is golden. Eat hot with maple or golden syrup.

For the lucky adults:
Replace the milk with 3 tablespoons of dry fino sherry. Cook as above. Then dip the fried bread in icing sugar mixed with ground cinnamon.

Dandelion Salad

Mix up well in a bowl.

a pinch of sugar

Crispy bacon in small pieces

Spoon over sugary dressing

Dandelion Salad

sugar
bacon
olive oil
salt & pepper
dandelion leaves.

See the photograph on page 62.
Wash 8 young dandelion leaves per person.
Pat them dry and tear them in half discarding
the stems. Put them in a salad bowl.

Snip 3 rashers of smoked streaky bacon per
person into squares using kitchen scissors.
Fry the bacon in 6 tablespoons of olive oil
until brown.

Sprinkle 1 spoon of sugar over the dandelion
leaves followed by the hot bacon and oil
from the frying pan. Mix it up well and then
season the salad with a little salt & pepper.

MORE EDIBLE FLOWERS AND
HOW TO USE THEM ....

A chocolate crispie with a primrose, recipe p. 65.

☆ **Primroses:** *(Primular vulgaris)* are too scarce to
gather in the wild unless they grow in great profusion.
They indicate the arrival of spring hence their name,
Primula, 'first rose' in Latin. They taste sweet and delicate.
Use them to decorate cakes or scatter on salad.

☆ **Alexanders:** abundant along coastal roadsides, the yellow flowers can be dipped in sugary batter and frittered or in salads.

☆ **Basil flowers:** taste milder than the leaves. Good for salads.

☆ **Broom: (***Cytisus scoparius***)** pick the soft bright yellow petals while still in bud. The pickled buds were a popular Elizabethan salad ingredient. Chef Hugh Fernley-Whittingstall uses them for wild tartar sauce and throws them into a vegetable stir fry.

☆ **Borage:** the blue star leaves are very decorative in drinks, salads or frozen into ice cubes, *see page 61.* They taste of mild cucumber as do the leaves and were believed to, 'lift the spirits'.

☆ **Cauliflower:** surprise surprise! It is a flower - as is Broccoli.

☆ **Chamomile:** the flowers in Spanish are called 'manzanilla' which means apple - alluding to their fragrance. Dry them for a sleep inducing infusion which has been drunk throughout time.

☆ **Capers:** the pickled flower-buds of the caper bush are one of my cupboard stalwarts. Throw into *beurre noire* for fish or pasta.

☆ **Chrysanthemums:** are used liberally in Japanese cooking where they are eaten with soy sauce. The flamboyant 'pom pom' flower inspires a national holiday. Sprinkle the petals over salads.

☆ **Chive flowers:** may be frittered. Dip them in a light tempura batter made by mixing egg white and a little water with rice flour.

☆ **Cloves:** the dried spice is the unexpanded flower bud of a clove tree. They absorb lots of moisture once picked. I use this spice in everything: curries, bread sauce, rice and puddings.

☆ **Common Mallow:** (*Malva sylvestris*) has edible leaves. The young shoots have been eaten since the 8th century. The pink streaked petals taste sweet scattered in salads. Marshmallow sweets used to be made from the starchy gelatinous roots.

☆ **Cornflowers:** (*Centaurea cyanus*) are edible and a very beautiful deep blue colour. Its' name derives from a Greek legend whereby the flowers covered the fatal wounds of Centaur Chiron.

☆ **Courgette** (*Cucurbita pepe)* **and Squash flowers:** are ideal for stuffing, battering and frying. Thus they are enjoyed by Europeans and Mexicans as a juicy culinary flower.

☆ **Cuckoo flower:** (*Cardamine pratensis*) is a relative of the watercress. Eat the leaves and flowers in salads. The springtime flowers range from lilac to white. They bloom when the cuckoo begins to sing in April and May hence the name of the plant.

☆ **Daisies** are not worth eating, but the leaves, fat and full of Vitamin C, are well worth slicing off the lawn to consume.

☆ **Fennel:** (*Foeniclum vulgarum*) chew the flowers as a breath sweetener and sprinkle them raw on salad. Fish cooked over dried and charred fennel stalks on an iron griddle tastes delicious. Stuff roast pork with fennel flowers and garlic. The refreshing flavour of the plant lends itself to sauces, sorbets & syrups. I use the chopped leaves in fennel mayonnaise for fish.

☆ **Gentian:** (*Gentiana nivalis*) the blue alpine flower is extremely bitter and yet very good for you. The flower is favoured by the French as a bitter aperitif and has been used medicinally for centuries. It is anti-inflamatory and stimulates blood production and appetite. Indigenous to England are the field gentian, autumn gentian and marsh gentian which have medicinal properties and are sadly, difficult to find nowadays.

☆ **False Acacia:** *(Robinia pseudocacia)* likes a mild climate and has a short flower season in the spring. Sprinkle the flowers in cognac and sugar. Leave for 30 minutes before frying in batter.

☆ **Field Scabious:** The pretty blue purple wild flower has diverse nutrients from its deep roots. It was for curing scabies.

☆ **Hibiscus:** flowers when dried are lemony tasting. Put them in champagne for dramatic colour or add boiling water for tea. Make the Egyptian cordial, *Karkadeeh* by adding 100g sugar to 100ml of hibiscus liquid - obtained by soaking it in water.

☆ **Jasmine:** (*jasmin officinale*) has a wonderful perfumed flavour. It makes a refreshing tea. Use it for steaming food.

☆ **Lilac:** use these fragrant mauve blossoms to decorate cakes.

☆ **Linden:** (lime) flower makes good tea, sweeten the 'Proustian '*Tilleul*' with honey. Bake the fragrant flowers with salmon as in p 35. The young leaves are edible in a sandwich.

☆ **Marigold:** was known as 'poor man's saffron'. Put the petals in egg sandwiches, bake them in buns, biscuits or lobster stew.

☆ **Meadowsweet:** flowers were a former flavouring for mead. In past times it was scattered over floors as a scent.

☆ **Carnation/Pinks:** (*Dianthus caryophyllus*) are very ancient and decorative flowers. The Elizabethans named them '*gillyfloure*'. The name 'carnation' stems from Latin for flesh - *carnis* - because of the colour. All the varieties of the pink or white soft raggedy petals are a 'feast for the eyes' and edible.

☆ **Pollen:** has loads of extraordinary properties. Memory improvement is just one! Its' mineral, *selenium* slows down ageing. Per weight it has more protein than any animal source.

☆ **Red Clover:** (*Trifolium pratense*) has an astonishing amount of Vitamin A (*1156 mg per 100g, Carrots = 2000 mg*). It is also one of the earliest cultivated plants and was esteemed by the Druids, Celts, Greeks and Romans; hence 'being in clover'. Fritter the flowers in tempura made from whisked egg white, iced water and rice flour.

☆ **Rosemary flowers:** were used to infuse honey in the 16th century. The flowers are decorative and milder than the pungent leaves which are an essential culinary herb most commonly eaten with lamb and roast potatoes but also befitting sweet dishes.

☆ **Saffron:** these *Crocus sativus* stamens are precious and expensive. The names derives from the Greek for yellow, *Zafran* in honour of its bright yellowy-orange colour. It is an impressive food dye and glaze. Originating in Persia by the 10th century it was a valuable trading commodity. In Cornwall it is eaten traditionally in sweet saffron cakes and buns. My favourite use is to add a few sprigs to a steaming pan of mussels. The black -blue of the shells and the orange saffron sauce looks stunning.

☆ **Scented Geranium:** seep the leaves in water overnight to make a sweet perfume flavour for sorbets and syrups. Leaves in the bottom of a cake tin makes an unusual tasting sponge cake.

☆ **Sweet Williams:** can be sprinkled over creamy pavlova topped with a flower flavoured cream and salty caramel sauce.

☆ **Tansy:** (*Chrysanthemum vulgare*) has cheerful yellow 'button' flowers. Historically the plant was used in the kitchen as an alternative to expensive imported spices such as nutmeg and cinnamon. A 'tansy' was a herb flavoured omelette. Because of its bitterness it is mostly used for medical purposes.

☆ **Thistle:** the peeled stem of this flower is edible raw or pickled

☆ **Thyme flowers:** may be infused to make a restorative tea.

☆ **Valerian:** the delicate white flowers were dried to make tea to help anxiety and to sooth shell-shocked soldiers after the war.

☆ **Violets:** adopted by the French Bonapartists because the flower's bloom coincided with the abdication of Napoleon in late March. He was nicknamed *Caporal Violet, 'the little flower that returns with Spring'*. Nowadays it is too scarce to be picked but Toulouse in France has a cultivated Violet industry and they are used for tea, biscuits and found crystalized on top of chocolates.

☆ **Violas:** are a good violet substitute sprinkled on crispy green salad, sugary pavlova or frozen into an ice flower bowl. *See page 61.*

FOOD FOR THOUGHT ...

"It is easy to forget, as one stands before the modern supermarket shelf, that every single one of the world's vegetable foods was once a wild plant". *Richard Mabey, 'Food for Free' 1972.*

"The instinct of foraging and hunting are deep within us all and we have lost much in failing to fulfill these needs". *John Wright, 'Edible Seashore' 2010.*

"One might argue that the internet has replaced the woods in terms of inventive space, but no electronic environment stimulates all the senses. So far Microsoft sells no match for nature's code". *Richard Louvre, 'The Last Child in the Woods,' 2008.*

"There is something wrong with a society that spends so much money, as well as countless hours of human effort - to make the least dregs of processed information available to everyone everywhere and yet does little or nothing to help us explore the world for ourselves". *Professor Edward Reed, 'The Necessity of Experience'.*

"... there is also the serendipity of harvesting wild foods. Unsought gifts abound ... The greatest unsought gift is that you become aware of the interdependency of plant, bird, beast and human". *Jean Craighead George 1982. 'Acorn Pancakes, Dandelion Salad & Recipes".*

"With the increase of populations and decrease of arable land and animal manure that kept it fertile, nations rely, more than ever on synthetic products denuded of minerals and vitamins." *P.T. Norris 1960, 'About Vitamins'.*

"When an Aboriginal mother notices the first stirrings of speech in her child, she lets it handle the 'things' of that particular country: leaves, fruit, insects and so forth.... We give our children guns and computer games. They gave their children the land". *Bruce Chatwin , 'The Songlines' 1987.*

"We must remember that food of better quality is food which has vitality, individuality, freshness; food which is grow right, not only food that looks right." *Lord Northbourne 1938, 'Look to the Land'.*

"A rule for survival is not to pass up any reasonable food sources if we are ever in need. There are many dead men who through ignorance or fastidiousness, did". *Bradford Angier, 'How to stay alive in the woods', 1956.*

To order further copies of *Eating Flowers*
please send the coupon below to:

Eating Flowers,
4 Dolphin Street,
Deal, Kent. UK. CT14 6LX

✂ -- - -- -

I enclose a UK bank cheque payable to:

Lucia Stuart for £10.00 per copy
including postage & packing.

NAME: ....

ADDRESS: ....

POSTCODE ....

Free UK Delivery. Please allow 28 days.
☎ 00 + 44 (0) 1304 369799

ISBN 978 0 9570974 0 7
www.eatingflowers.com